OBSCENITY AND INDECENCY: CONSTITUTIONAL PRINCIPLES AND FEDERAL STATUTES

OBSCENITY AND INDECENCY: CONSTITUTIONAL PRINCIPLES AND FEDERAL STATUTES

HENRY COHEN

Novinka Books
New York

Senior Editors: Susan Boriotti and Donna Dennis
Coordinating Editor: Tatiana Shohov
Office Manager: Annette Hellinger
Graphics: Wanda Serrano
Editorial Production: Vladimir Klestov, Matthew Kozlowski, Tom Moceri, Anthony T. Sovak, Alexandra Columbus and Maya Columbus
Circulation: Ave Maria Gonzalez, Vera Popovic, Luis Aviles, Raymond Davis, Melissa Diaz, Marlene Nunez and Jeannie Pappas
Communications and Acquisitions: Serge P. Shohov
Marketing: Cathy DeGregory

Library of Congress Cataloging-in-Publication Data

ISBN: 1-59033-749-2

Nova Science Publishers, Inc.
400 Oser Ave, Suite 1600
Hauppauge, New York 11788-3619
Tele. 631-231-7269 Fax 631-231-8175
e-mail: Novascience@earthlink.net
Web Site: http://www.novapublishers.com

Printed in the United States of America

CONTENTS

PREFACE

The First Amendment provides: "Congress shall make no law ... abridging the freedom of speech, or of the press." In general, the First Amendment protects pornography, with this term being used to mean any erotic material. The Supreme Court, however, has held that the First Amendment does not protect two types of pornography: obscenity and child pornography. Consequently, they may be banned on the basis of their content, and federal law prohibits the mailing of obscenity, as well as its transport or receipt in interstate or foreign commerce.

Most pornography is not legally obscene; to be obscene, pornography must, at a minimum, "depict or describe patently offensive 'hard core' sexual conduct." The Supreme Court has created a three-part test, known as the *Miller* test, to determine whether a work is obscene. Pornography that is not obscene may not be banned, but may be regulated as to the time, place, and manner of its distribution, particularly in order to keep it from children. Thus, the courts have upheld the zoning and licensing of pornography dealers, as well as restrictions on dial-a-porn, nude dancing, and indecent radio and television broadcasting.

Federal statutes, in addition to making it a crime to mail obscenity or to transport or receive it in interstate or foreign commerce, provide for criminal and civil forfeiture of real and personal property used in making obscenity pornography, and of the profits of obscenity — in some instances even when they were already used to pay a third party. In addition, obscenity crimes are included among the predicate offenses that may give rise to a violation of the Federal Racketeer Influenced and Corrupt Organizations Act (RICO).

The Internet has given rise to three federal statutes designed to protect minors from sexual material posted on it. The Communications Decency Act of 1996 makes it a crime knowingly to use a telecommunications device (telephone, fax, or e-mail) to make an obscene or indecent communication to a minor, or knowingly to use an interactive computer service to transmit an obscene communication to anyone or an indecent communication to a minor. The Supreme Court, however, held the inclusion of "indecent" communications in this statute unconstitutional. Congress, therefore, enacted the less-broad Child Online Protection Act (COPA) , the constitutionality of which has also been challenged. Finally, the Children's Internet Protection Act (CIPA), enacted at the end of the 106th Congress, requires schools and libraries that accept federal funds to purchase computers or Internet access to block or filter obscenity, child pornography, and, with respect to minors, material that is "harmful to minors." In May, 2002, a three-judge federal district court held CIPA unconstitutional on the ground that "the filtering software mandated by CIPA will block access to substantial amounts of constitutionally protected speech." In November, 2002, the Supreme Court agreed to review the CIPA case. Both COPA and CIPA have been enjoined from being enforced.

Chapter 1

CONSTITUTIONAL PRINCIPLES

To be constitutional, a federal statute must be enacted pursuant to a power of Congress enumerated in the Constitution and must not contravene any provision of the Constitution. Two powers enumerated in Article I, Section 8 of the Constitution give Congress the power to enact statutes regulating or banning pornography: the power "To regulate Commerce with foreign Nations, and among the several States," and the power "To establish Post Offices and post Roads." Thus, Congress may enact statutes, provided they do not contravene any provision of the Constitution, that regulate pornography that crosses state or national boundaries, is imported or exported, or is mailed.

The provision of the Constitution that federal statutes regulating pornography are most likely to be in danger of contravening is the First Amendment's provision that "Congress shall make no law ... abridging the freedom of speech, or of the press."[1] Although pornography in general is protected by the First Amendment, two types of pornography — obscenity and child pornography — are not.[2] Therefore, pornography that does not constitute obscenity or child pornography may ordinarily be regulated only with respect to its time, place, and manner of distribution.[3] An outright ban

---

1 Despite its mentioning only "Congress," the First Amendment applies equally to all branches of the federal government and the states. Herbert v. Lando, 441 U.S. 153, 168 n.16 (1979).

2 Child pornography is material that visually depicts sexual conduct by children. New York v. Ferber, 458 U.S. 747, 764 (1982). It is unprotected by the First Amendment even when it is not legally obscene; *i.e.*, child pornography need not meet the *Miller* test to be banned. For additional information, *see*, *Child Pornography: Constitutional Principles and Federal Statutes* (CRS Report 95-406 A).

3 In *Frisby v. Schultz*, 487 U.S. 474, 481 (1988), the Supreme Court noted: "The State may ... enforce regulations of the time, place, and manner of expression which are contentneutral

on pornography other than obscenity or child pornography would violate the First Amendment unless it served "to promote a compelling interest" and was "the least restrictive means to further the articulated interest."[4] Obscenity and child pornography, however, being without First Amendment protection, may be totally banned on the basis of their content, not only in the absence of a compelling governmental interest, but in the absence of any evidence of harm.

Obscenity apparently is unique in being the only type of speech to which the Supreme Court has denied First Amendment protection without regard to whether it can cause harm. According to the Court, there is evidence that, at the time of the adoption of the First Amendment, obscenity "was outside the protection intended for speech and press."[5] Consequently, obscenity may be banned simply because a legislature concludes that banning it protects "the social interest in order and morality."[6]

A. The Miller Test

Most pornography is not legally obscene; *i.e.*, most pornography is protected by the First Amendment. To be obscene, pornography must, at a minimum, "depict or describe patently offensive 'hard core' sexual conduct."[7] The Supreme Court has created a three-part test, known as the *Miller* test, to determine whether a work is obscene. The *Miller* test asks:

> (a) whether the "average person applying contemporary community standards" would find that the work, taken as a whole, appeals to the prurient interest; (b) whether the work depicts or describes, in a patently offensive way, sexual conduct specifically defined by the applicable state

---

[*i.e.*, "are *justified* without reference to the content of the speech," *Renton v. Playtime Theaters, Inc.*, 475 U.S. 41, 48 (1986) (emphasis in original)], are narrowly tailored to serve a significant [not necessarily a compelling] government interest, and leave open ample alternative channels of communication [but need not necessarily be the least restrictive means to further the government interest]."

4 Sable Communications of California v. Federal Communications Commission, 492 U.S. 115, 126 (1989).

5 Roth v. United States, 354 U.S. 476, 483 (1957). However, Justice Douglas, dissenting, wrote: "[T]here is no special historical evidence that literature dealing with sex was intended to be treated in a special manner by those who drafted the First Amendment." *Id.* at 514.

6 *Id.* at 485.

7 Miller v. California, 413 U.S. 15, 27 (1973).

law; and (c) whether the work, taken as a whole, lacks serious literary, artistic, political, or scientific value.[8]

In *Pope v. Illinois*, the Supreme Court clarified that "the first and second prongs of the *Miller* test — appeal to prurient interest and patent offensiveness — are issues of fact for the jury to determine applying contemporary community standards."[9] However, as for the third prong, "[t]he proper inquiry is not whether an ordinary member of any given community would find serious literary, artistic, political, or scientific value in allegedly obscene material, but whether a reasonable person would find such value in the material, taken as a whole."[10]

When a federal statute refers to "obscenity," it should be understood to refer only to pornography that is obscene under the *Miller* standard, as application of the statute to other material would ordinarily be

---

8 *Id.* at 24 (citation omitted). In *Brockett v. Spokane Arcades, Inc.*, 472 U.S. 491, 498 (1984), the Court struck down a state statute to the extent that it defined "prurient" as "that which incites lasciviousness or lust." The Court held that a publication was not obscene if it "provoked only normal, healthy sexual desires." To be obscene it must appeal to "a shameful or morbid interest in nudity, sex, or excretion." In *Manual Enterprises v. Day*, 370 U.S. 478, 480 (1962), the Court indicated that photographs of nude male models, although they appealed to the prurient interest and lacked literary, scientific, or other merit, were not patently offensive merely because they were aimed at homosexuals. In *Jenkins v. Georgia*, 418 U.S. 153, 160 (1974), the Court held that the film "Carnal Knowledge" was not obscene, writing: "Even though questions of appeal to the 'prurient interest' or of patent offensiveness are 'essentially questions of fact,' it would be a serious misreading of *Miller* to conclude that juries have unbridled discretion in determining what is 'patently offensive.'" In *Jacobellis v. Ohio*, 378 U.S. 184, 197 (1964), Justice Stewart, concurring, noted that "criminal laws in this area are constitutionally limited to hard-core pornography, which he would not attempt to define. Then followed his famous remark: "But I know it when I see it, and the motion picture involved in this case is not that." The motion picture was a French film called "Les Amants" ("The Lovers").

9 481 U.S. 497, 500 (1987). In *Hamling v. United States*, 418 U.S. 87, 105 (1974), the Court noted that a "community" was not any "precise geographic area," and suggested that it might be less than an entire state. In *Jenkins v. Georgia*, *supra* note 8, 418 U.S., at 157 (1974), the Court approved a "trial court's instructions directing jurors to apply 'community standards' without specifying what 'community.'"

10 Justice Scalia concurred in the result in *Pope v. Illinois*, but wrote: "[I]n my view it is quite impossible to come to an objective assessment of (at least) literary or artistic value, there being many accomplished people who have found literature in Dada, and art in the replication of a soup can. Since ratiocination has little to do with esthetics, the fabled 'reasonable man' is of little help in the inquiry, and would have to be replaced with, perhaps, the 'man of tolerably good taste' — a description that betrays the lack of an ascertainable standard.... I think we would be better advised to adopt as a legal maxim what has long been the wisdom of mankind: *De gustibus non est disputandum*. Just as there is no arguing about taste, there is no use litigating about it." *Id.* at 504-505.

unconstitutional.[11] However, narrowly drawn statutes that serve a compelling interest, such as protecting minors, may be permissible even if they restrict pornography that is not obscene under *Miller*.[12] In *Sable Communications of California, Inc. v. Federal Communications Commission*, the Supreme Court

> recognized that there is a compelling interest in protecting the physical and psychological well-being of minors. This interest extends to shielding minors from the influence of literature that is not obscene by adult standards. The government may serve this legitimate interest, but to withstand constitutional scrutiny, "it must do so by narrowly drawn regulations without unnecessarily interfering with First Amendment freedoms." It is not enough to show that the government's ends are compelling; the means must be carefully tailored to achieved those ends.[13]

In *Sable*, the Supreme Court applied these principles to the government's attempt to proscribe dial-a-porn; see below.

The Supreme Court has allowed one exception to the rule that obscenity, as defined by *Miller*, is not protected under the First Amendment. In *Stanley v. Georgia*, the Court held that "mere private possession of obscene material" is protected. The Court wrote:

---

[11] "When the validity of an act of the Congress is drawn in question, and even if a serious doubt of constitutionality is raised, it is a cardinal principle that this Court will first ascertain whether a construction of the statute is fairly possible by which the question may be avoided." Crowell v. Benson, 285 U.S. 22, 62 (1932).

[12] In *Federal Communications Commission v. Pacifica Foundation*, 438 U.S. 726, 749-750 (1978), the Supreme Court, upholding the power of the Federal Communications Commission to regulate a radio broadcast that was "indecent" but not obscene, wrote:

> We held in *Ginsberg v. New York*, 390 U.S. 629, that the government's interest in the "well-being of its youth" and in supporting "parents' claim to authority in their own household" justified the regulation of otherwise protected expression. *Id.*, at 640 and 639. The ease with which children may obtain access to broadcast material, coupled with the concerns recognized in *Ginsberg*, amply justify special treatment of indecent broadcasting.

In *Reno v. American Civil Liberties Union*, 521 U.S. 844, 878 (1997), the Supreme Court suggested that the strength of the government's interest in protecting minors may vary depending upon the age of the minor, the parental control, and the artistic or educational value of the material in question.

[13] 492 U.S. 115, 126 (1989) (citations omitted). It might appear that regulations could be "narrowly drawn" or "carefully tailored" without being the "least restrictive means" to further a governmental interest. But *Sable*, on the same page, also uses the latter phrase (quoted above in the text accompanying note 4), and the Court has elsewhere made clear that the "narrow tailoring" required for content-based restrictions is more stringent than that required for time, place, and manner restrictions (*see*, note 3, *supra*), where "leastrestrictive-alternative analysis is wholly out of place." Ward v. Rock Against Racism, 491 U.S. 781, 798-799 n.6 (1989).

> Whatever may be the justifications for other statutes regulating obscenity, we do not think they reach into the privacy of one's own home. If the First Amendment means anything, it means that a State has no business telling a man, sitting alone in his house, what books he may read or what films he may watch.[14]

Subsequently, however, the Supreme Court rejected the claim that under *Stanley* there is a constitutional right to provide obscene material for private use,[15] or to acquire it for private use.[16] The right to possess obscene material does not imply the right to provide or acquire it, because the right to possess it "reflects no more than ... the law's 'solicitude to protect the privacies of the life within [the home].'"[17]

B. Zoning and Licensing of Pornography Dealers

In *Young v. American Mini Theaters, Inc.*, the Supreme Court held that "[t]he mere fact that the commercial exploitation of material protected by the First Amendment is subject to zoning and other licensing requirements is not a sufficient reason for invalidating these ordinances."[18] In *Young*, the Court upheld ordinances that required dispersal of "adult" establishments; specifically, the ordinances provided that an adult theater could not be located within 1,000 feet of any two other "regulated uses" (adult bookstores, cabarets, bars, hotels, etc.) or within 500 feet of a residential area. In *Renton v. Playtime Theaters, Inc.,* the Court upheld an ordinance that required that adult theaters be concentrated in limited areas; it prohibited adult "theaters from locating within 1,000 feet of any residential zone, singleor multiple-family dwelling, church, park, or school."[19]

In *Young*, the Court reasoned that

---

14 394 U.S. 557, 565, 568 (1969). The Court has held that there is no right even to private possession of child pornography. Osborne v. Ohio, 495 U.S. 103 (1990).

15 United States v. Reidel, 402 U.S. 351 (1971).

16 United States v. 12 200-Ft. Reels of Film, 413 U.S. 123 (1973).

17 *Id.* at 127. *See*, Edwards, *Obscenity in the Age of Direct Broadcast Satellite: A Final Burial for* Stanley v. Georgia*(?), a National Obscenity Standard, and Other Miscellany*, 33 William and Mary Law Review 949 (1992).

18 427 U.S. 50, 62 (1976).

19 475 U.S. 41, 43 (1986).

> what is ultimately at stake is nothing more than a limitation on the place where adult films may be exhibited, even though the determination of whether a particular film fits that characterization turns on the nature of its content... . The situation would be quite different if the ordinance had the effect of suppressing, or greatly restricting access to, lawful speech.[20]

In *Renton*, the Court wrote:

> The ordinance by its terms is designed to prevent crime, protect the city's retail trade, maintain property values, and generally "protec[t] and preserv[e] the quality of [the city's] neighborhoods, commercial districts, and the quality of urban life," not to suppress the expression of unpopular views... . In short, the Renton ordinance is completely consistent with our definition of "contentneutral" speech regulations as those that "are *justified* without reference to the content of the regulated speech."[21]

In both *Young* and *Renton*, the Court found the ordinances in question to be narrow enough to affect only those theaters shown to produce the unwanted secondary effects, such as crime.[22] In this respect they were unlike the regulations the Court struck down as overbroad in two other cases. In *Erznoznik v. City of Jacksonville*, the ordinance prohibited drive-in theaters from showing films containing nudity when the screen was visible from a public street.[23] In *Schad v. Mount Ephraim*, the ordinance prohibited live entertainment from a broad range of commercial uses permitted in a commercial zone; the ordinance in this case was used to prosecute an adult bookstore that featured coin-operated booths that permitted customers to watch nude dancing.[24]

In *FW/PBS, Inc. v. Dallas*, the Supreme Court considered a challenge to a city ordinance that regulated "sexually oriented businesses through a scheme incorporating zoning, licensing, and inspections," and prohibited "individuals convicted of certain crimes from obtaining a license to operate a sexually oriented business for a specified period of years."[25] The ordinance defined a "sexually oriented business" as "an adult arcade, adult bookstore or adult video store, adult cabaret, adult motel, adult motion picture theater,

---

[20] *Young*, *supra* note 18, at 71-72 n.35.

[21] *Renton*, *supra* note 19, at 48 (emphasis in original).

[22] 427 U.S. at 71; 475 U.S. at 52.

[23] 422 U.S. 205 (1975).

[24] 452 U.S. 61 (1981).

[25] 493 U.S. 215 (1990).

escort agency, nude model studio, or sexual encounter center."[26] The Court held that the licensing scheme

> does not provide for an effective limitation on the time within which the licensor's decision must be made. It also fails to provide an avenue for prompt judicial review so as to minimize suppression of the speech in the event of a license denial. We therefore hold that the failure to provide these essential safeguards renders the ordinance's licensing requirement unconstitutional insofar as it is enforced against those businesses engaged in First Amendment activity... [27]

One type of business covered by the ordinance that was not engaged in First Amendment activity was adult motels, which the ordinance defined as motels that rented rooms for less than 10 hours. Inclusion of these motels was challenged on two grounds: (1) that the city had "violated the Due Process Clause by failing to produce adequate support for its supposition that renting rooms for less than 10 hours results in increased crime or other secondary effects," and (2) "that the 10-hour limitation on the rental of motel rooms places an unconstitutional burden on the right to freedom of association ... ."[28]

The Court rejected both arguments. As for the first, it found "it reasonable to believe that shorter rental time periods indicate that the motels foster prostitution."[29] As for the second, it found that the associations "that are formed from the use of a motel room for less than 10 hours are not those that have 'played a critical role in the culture and traditions of the Nation by cultivating and transmitting shared ideals and beliefs.'"[30]

In *Los Angeles v. Alameda Books, Inc.*, the Supreme Court reversed a grant of summary judgment that had struck down a municipal ordinance that prohibited "the establishment or maintenance of more than one adult entertainment business in the same building, structure or portion thereof."[31] A federal district court had granted summary judgment and the Court of Appeals for the Ninth Circuit had affirmed on the ground "that the city failed to present evidence upon which it could reasonably rely to demonstrate a link between multiple-use adult establishments and negative secondary

---

26 *Id.* at 220.

27 *Id.* at 229.

28 *Id.* at 236-237.

29 *Id.* at 236.

30 *Id.* at 237.

31 122 S. Ct. 1728, 1731 (2002).

effects."[32] The Supreme Court reversed, finding that the city "may reasonably rely on a study it conducted some years before enacting the present version of § 12.70(C) to demonstrate that its ban on multiple-use adult establishments serves its interest in reducing crime."[33] It therefore remanded the case so that the city would have the opportunity to demonstrate this at trial.

The four-judge plurality opinion in *Alameda Books* "held that a municipality may rely on any evidence that is 'reasonably believed to be relevant' for demonstrating a causal connection between speech and a substantial, independent governmental interest," such as reducing crime or maintaining property values.[34] Justice Kennedy, whose concurring opinion was necessary for a majority, added that, not only must the city demonstrate that its ordinance will "suppress secondary effects"; it must also demonstrate that it will leave "the quantity and accessibility of speech substantially intact."[35] The four dissenting justices found that "the city has failed to show any causal relationship between the breakup policy and elimination or regulation of secondary effects," and, therefore, that summary judgment had been properly granted.[36]

C. Nude Dancing

The Supreme Court has twice upheld the application of laws banning public nudity to nudity in "adult" entertainment establishments where the viewers are all consenting adults who have paid to see the dancers. In *Barnes v. Glen Theatre, Inc.*, the Supreme Court held that the First Amendment does not prevent the government from requiring that dancers wear "pasties" and a "G-string" when they dance (nonobscenely) in such establishments.[37] Indiana sought to enforce a state statute prohibiting public nudity against two such establishments, which asserted First Amendment protection. The Court found that the statute proscribed public nudity across the board, not nude dancing as such, and therefore imposed only an incidental restriction on expression. A statute that is intended to suppress speech will be upheld only

---

[32] *Id.*
[33] *Id.*
[34] *Id.* at 1736.
[35] *Id.* at 1742.
[36] *Id.* at 1747.
[37] 501 U.S. 560 (1991).

if it serves a compelling governmental interest and is the least restrictive means to further that interest. By contrast, under *United States v. O'Brien*, a statute that imposes an incidental restriction, like one that imposes a time, place, or manner restriction, will be upheld if it is narrowly tailored to further a substantial, but not necessarily compelling, governmental interest.[38]

There was no majority opinion in the case. Justice Rehnquist, joined by Justices O'Connor and Kennedy, found the statute no more restrictive than necessary to further the governmental interest of "protecting societal order and morality."[39] Justice Souter found the relevant governmental interest to be "combating the secondary effects of adult entertainment establishments," such as prostitution, sexual assaults, and other criminal activity.[40] The fifth Justice necessary to uphold the nude dancing prohibition, Justice Scalia, thought that the case raised no First Amendment issue at all, because the incidental restriction was on conduct, not speech, and "virtually *every* law restricts conduct, and virtually *any* prohibited conduct can be performed for expressive purposes."[41] Four Justices dissented, finding insufficient "the plurality and Justice Scalia's simple references to the State's general interest in promoting societal order and morality ... . The purpose of forbidding people to appear nude in parks, beaches, hot dog stands, and like public places is to protect others from offense. But that could not possibly be the purpose of preventing nude dancing in theaters and barrooms since the viewers are exclusively consenting adults who paid money to see these dances. The purpose of the proscription in these contexts is to protect the viewers from what the State believes is the harmful message that nude dancing communicates."[42] This purpose is impermissible under the First Amendment.

In *Erie v. Pap's A.M.*, the Supreme Court again upheld the application of a statute prohibiting public nudity to an "adult" entertainment establishment.[43] Although there was again only a plurality opinion, this time by Justice O'Connor, Parts I and II of that opinion were joined by five justices. These five adopted Justice Souter's position in *Barnes*, that the statute satisfied the *O'Brien* test because it was intended "to combat harmful secondary effects," such as "prostitution and other criminal activity."[44]

---

[38] 391 U.S. 367 (1968).

[39] *Barnes*, *supra* note 37, at 568.

[40] *Id.* at 582.

[41] *Id.* at 576 (emphasis in original).

[42] *Id.* at 590-591 (White, J., dissenting, joined by Justices Marshall, Blackmun, and Stevens).

[43] 529 U.S. 277. (2000).

[44] *Id.* at 292, 291.

Justice Souter, however, though joining the plurality opinion, also dissented in part in *Erie*. He continued to believe that secondary effects were an adequate justification for banning nude dancing, but did not believe "that the city has made a sufficient evidentiary showing to sustain its regulation," and therefore would have remanded the case for further proceedings.[45] He acknowledged his "mistake" in *Barnes* in failing to make the same demand for evidence.[46]

The plurality opinion in *Erie* found that the effect of Erie's public nudity ban "on the erotic message ... is *de minimis*" because Erie allows dancers to perform wearing only pasties and G-strings.[47] It may follow that "requiring dancers to wear pasties and G-strings may not greatly reduce ... secondary effects, but *O'Brien* requires only that the regulation further the interest of combating such effects," not that it further it to a particular extent.[48] Justice Scalia, this time joined by Justice Thomas, again took the view that, "[w]hen conduct other than speech itself is regulated ... the First Amendment is violated only '[w]here the government prohibits conduct precisely because of its communicative attributes.'"[49] He found, therefore, that the statute should be upheld without regard to "secondary effects," but simply as an attempt "to foster good morals."[50]

Justice Stevens, dissenting in *Erie* and joined by Justice Ginsburg, wrote: "Until now, the 'secondary effects' of commercial enterprises featuring indecent entertainment have justified only the regulation of their location. For the first time, the Court has now held that such effects may justify the total suppression of protected speech. Indeed, the plurality opinion concludes that admittedly trivial advancements of a State's interest may provide the basis for censorship."[51] It concludes, that is, that the *O'Brien*

---

45 *Id.* at 310-311.

46 *Id.* at 1405.

47 *Id.* at 316. The plurality said that, though nude dancing is "expressive conduct" [which ordinarily means it would be entitled to full First Amendment protection], "we think that it falls only within the outer ambit of the First Amendment's protection." *Id.* at 289. The opinion also quotes Justice Stevens to the same effect with regard to erotic materials generally. *Id.* at 294. In *United States v. Playboy Entertainment Group, Inc.*, *infra* note 100, 529 U.S., at 826, however, the Court wrote that it "cannot be influenced ... by the perception that the regulation in question is not a major one because the speech is not very important."

48 *Id.* at 301.

49 *Id.* at 310.

50 *Id.*

51 *Id.* at 317-318.

"test can be satisfied by nothing more than the mere possibility of *de minimis* effects on the neighborhood."[52]

The plurality in *Erie* did not address the question of whether statutes prohibiting public nudity could be applied to ban serious theater that contains nudity. In *Barnes*, Justice Souter wrote: "It is difficult to see ... how the enforcement of Indiana's statute against nudity in a production of 'Hair' or 'Equus' somewhere other than an 'adult' theater would further the State's interest in avoiding harmful secondary effects ... ."[53]

---

[52] *Id.* at 324. Justice Stevens also wrote that the plurality was "mistaken in equating our secondary effects cases with the 'incidental burdens' doctrine applied in cases such as *O'Brien...* . The incidental burdens doctrine applies when speech and non-speech elements are combined in the same course of conduct"[internal quotation marks omitted], whereas secondary effects "are indirect consequences of protected speech." *Id.*

[53] *Barnes*, *supra* note 37, 501 U.S., at 585 n.2.

Chapter 2

FEDERAL OBSCENITY AND INDECENCY STATUTES

A. POSTAL SERVICE PROVISIONS

Sections 3008 and 3010 of Title 39 allow people to prevent mail that they find offensive from being sent to them. Section 3008 provides that a person who receives in the mail "any pandering advertisement which offers for sale matter which the addressee in his sole discretion believes to be erotically arousing or sexually provocative" may request the Postal Service to issue an order directing the sender to refrain from further mailings to the addressee, and the Postal Service must do so. If the Postal Service believes that a sender has violated such an order, it may request the Attorney General to apply to a federal court for an order directing compliance.

The language of 39 U.S.C. § 3008 is broad enough to apply to any unwanted advertisement, regardless of content, as the Supreme Court indicated in upholding the constitutionality of the statute. "We ... categorically reject," the Court said, "the argument that a vendor has a right under the Constitution or otherwise to send unwanted material into the home of another."[1]

Section 3010 provides that any person may file with the Postal Service a statement "that he desires to receive no sexually oriented advertisements through the mails." The Postal Service shall make the list available, and "[n]o person shall mail or cause to be mailed any sexually oriented advertisement to any individual whose name and address has been on the list

---

1 Rowan v. Post Office Department, 397 U.S. 728, 738 (1970).

for more than 30 days." Section 3011 provides that, if the Postal Service believes that any person is violating section 3010, it may request the Attorney General to commence a civil action against such person in a federal district court. The court may employ various remedies to prevent future mailings.

Violations of sections 3008 and 3010 are also subject to criminal penalties under 18 U.S.C. § 1737.

B. Dial-a-Porn

The federal law concerning dial-a-porn is section 223(b) of the Communications Act of 1934, as amended, 47 U.S.C. § 223(b). Prior to April 1988, it banned both obscene and indecent dial-a-porn in interstate commerce and foreign communications, but only if it involved persons under eighteen. Although pornography that is indecent but not obscene is protected by the First Amendment, restricting minors' access to pornography, even to non-obscene pornography, generally presents no constitutional problems, as minors do not have the same rights as adults under the First Amendment.

Therefore, the pre-April 1988 version of section 223(b) apparently was constitutional. In April 1988, however, P.L. 100-297, § 6101, amended section 223(b) to ban obscene and indecent dial-a-porn in interstate and foreign communications, whether involving adults or children.

In June 1989, the Supreme Court declared section 223(b) unconstitutional insofar as it applies to indecent messages that are not obscene.[2] The Court noted "that while the Government has a legitimate interest in protecting children from exposure to indecent dial-a-porn messages, § 223(b) was not sufficiently narrowly drawn to serve that purpose and thus violated the First Amendment."[3] "[C]redit card, access code, and scrambling rules ... [would have] represented a 'feasible and effective' way to serve the Government's compelling interest in protecting children."[4] The government argued that these methods "would not be effective enough," but the Court found "no evidence in the record ... to that effect ... ."[5] The Court concluded:

2 Sable Communications of California, Inc. v. F.C.C., *supra* note 4, 492 U.S. 115 (1989).

3 *Id.* at 126

4 *Id.* at 128.

5 *Id.*

> Because the statute's denial of adult access to telephone messages which are indecent but not obscene far exceeds that which is necessary to limit the access of minors to such messages, we hold that the ban does not survive constitutional scrutiny.[6]

The upshot of *Sable* was that Congress' 1988 extension to adults of the ban on dial-a-porn that is indecent but not obscene resulted in federal law's not banning such dial-a-porn at all, even if used by minors. Section 223(b) after the decision banned dial-a-porn only if it was obscene.

Therefore, in 1989, Congress enacted P.L. 101-166, known as the "Helms Amendment," which amended section 223(b) to ban indecent dial-a-porn, if used by persons under 18. Under the 1988 law, section 223(b) applied "in the District of Columbia or in interstate or foreign communications"; under the Helms Amendment, it applies to all calls "within the United States."

The Helms Amendment also added section 223(c), which prohibits telephone companies, "to the extent technically feasible," from providing access to any dial-a-porn "from the telephone of any subscriber who has not previously requested [it] in writing ... ." In order to enable telephone companies to comply with this provision, Federal Communications Commission regulations require dial-a-porn providers to give written notice to the telephone company that they are providing indecent communications. 47 C.F.R. § 64.201.[7]

The Helms Amendment was challenged as unconstitutional, but a federal court of appeals upheld it, and the Supreme Court declined to review the case.[8] The court of appeals found that the word "indecent" as used in the statute was not void for vagueness,[9] that the statute was the least restrictive

---

6 *Id.* at 131.

7 Section 223(b) provides that a person found guilty of knowingly communicating *obscene* dial-a-porn "shall be fined in accordance with title 18 of the United States Code, or imprisoned not more than two years, or both." Title 18, § 3571, provides for fines of up to $250,000 for individuals and up to $500,000 for organizations. A person found guilty of knowingly communicating *indecent* dial-a-porn "shall be fined not more than $50,000 or imprisoned not more than six months, or both." Section 223(b) also provides for additional fines.

8 Dial Information Services Corp. v. Thornburgh, 938 F.2d 1535 (2d Cir. 1991), *cert. denied*, 502 U.S. 1072 (1992).

9 The court noted that the word has been "defined clearly" by the Federal Communications Commission, in the dial-a-porn context, "as the description or depiction of sexual or excretory activities or organs in a patently offensive manner as measured by contemporary community standards for the telephone medium." 938 F.2d, at 1540. The court noted that this definition tracks the one quoted in note 70, *infra*. *Id.* at 1541.

means to achieve a compelling governmental interest,[10] and that the requirement that the dial-a-porn provider inform the telephone company that its message was indecent did not constitute prior restraint.

C. OBSCENITY PROVISIONS AT 18 U.S.C. §§ 1460-1470

Federal law contains no outright ban on all obscenity; it leaves this to state law. However, the following federal statutes prohibit, among other things, obscenity on federal land or in federal buildings, in the mail, on radio and television, in interstate or foreign commerce, and on interstate highways and railroads even when the obscene material is transported intrastate.

Section 1460

This section makes it a crime, "in the special maritime and territorial jurisdiction of the United States or on any land or building owned by, leased to, or otherwise used by or under the control of the Government of the United States," or "in the Indian country as defined in section 1151 of this title," to sell or to possess with intent to sell, any obscene visual depiction.

Section 1461

This section declares to be "nonmailable matter" any "obscene, lewd, lascivious, indecent, filthy, or vile article, matter, thing, device, or substance," and makes it a crime knowingly to mail nonmailable matter. This statute should be read to prohibit only what constitutionally may be prohibited.[11]

Section 1462

This section prohibits importation of, and interstate or foreign transportation of, "any obscene, lewd, lascivious, or filthy" printed matter,

---

[10] *Id.* at 1541-1543; *see*, text accompanying note 4, *supra*.

[11] *See*, United States v. Merrill, 746 F.2d 458 (9th Cir. 1984), *cert. denied*, 469 U.S. 1165 (1985).

film, or sound recording, "or other matter of indecent character." The Supreme Court has written that, if and when serious doubt is raised as to the vagueness of the terms used in section 1462,

> we are prepared to construe such terms as limiting regulated material to patently offensive representations or descriptions of that specific "hard core" sexual conduct given as examples in *Miller* v. *California*, *ante*, at 25... . Of course, Congress could always define other specific "hard core" conduct.[12]

In 1996, P.L. 104-104, § 507(a), amended 18 U.S.C. § 1462 to apply to any "interactive computer service."

Section 1463

This section prohibits mailing matter, "upon the envelope or outside cover or wrapper of which, and all postal cards, upon which, any delineations, epithets, terms, or language of an indecent, lewd, lascivious, or obscene character are written or printed or otherwise impressed or apparent." Under this provision, "language of an 'indecent' character must be equated with language of an 'obscene' character" (and does not include "writing [on a post card] that a female runs around a dwelling house naked").[13]

Section 1464

This section provides, in full:

> Whoever utters any obscene, indecent, or profane language by means of radio communication shall be fined under this title or imprisoned not more than two years, or both.[14]

---

[12] United States v. 12 200-Ft. Reels of Film, 413 U.S. 123, 130 n.7 (1973).

[13] United States v. Keller, 259 F.2d 54, 57, 58 (3d Cir. 1958).

[14] This statute dates back to section 326 of the Communications Act of 1934, 48 Stat. 1091, which is why it uses only the term "radio." The term "radio," however, today includes broadcast television; *i.e.*, television transmitted over radio waves. In dictum, the Supreme Court noted that "the televising of nudes might well raise a serious question of programming contrary to 18 U.S.C. § 1464... ." F.C.C. v. Pacifica Foundation, 438 U.S. 726, 741 n.16 (1978); *see also*, *id.* at 750. "Radio communication" is defined for purposes of Title 47, U.S. Code, to mean "the transmission by radio of writing, signs, signals, *pictures*, and sounds of all kinds ... ." 47 U.S.C. § 153(b) (emphasis added).

This statute, unlike the others cited thus far, may be applied to language that is not obscene under *Miller*. This is because broadcasting has more limited First Amendment protection than other media. As the Supreme Court explained in *Red Lion Broadcasting Co. v. Federal Communications Commission*:

> Where there are substantially more individuals who want to broadcast than there are frequencies to allocate, it is idle to posit an unabridgeable First Amendment right to broadcast comparable to the right of every individual to speak, write, or publish.[15]

In *Federal Communications Commission v. Pacifica Foundation*, the FCC had taken action against a radio station for broadcasting a recording of George Carlin's "Filthy Words" monologue at 2 p.m., and the station had claimed First Amendment protection.[16] The Supreme Court upheld the power of the FCC under § 1464 "to regulate a radio broadcast that is indecent but not obscene."[17] The Court cited two distinctions between broadcasting and other media: "First, the broadcast media have established a uniquely pervasive presence in the lives of all Americans ... confront[ing] the citizen, not only in public, but also in the privacy of the home ... ," and "Second, broadcasting is uniquely accessible to children ... ."[18]

Nevertheless, the broadcast media have some First Amendment protection, and the Court emphasized the narrowness of its holding:

> The Commission's decision rested entirely on a nuisance rationale under which context is all-important. The concept requires consideration of a host of variables. The time of day was emphasized by the Commission... .[19]

---

15 395 U.S. 367, 388 (1969). In this case, the Supreme Court upheld the constitutionality of the Federal Communication Commission's "fairness doctrine," which required broadcast media licensees to provide coverage of controversial issues of interest to the community and to provide a reasonable opportunity for the presentation of contrasting viewpoints on such issues.

16 438 U.S. 726 (1978).

17 *Id.* at 729. The Court stated that, to be indecent, a broadcast need not have prurient appeal; "the normal definition of 'indecent' merely refers to nonconformance with accepted standards of morality." *Id.* at 740. The FCC holds that the concept "is intimately connected with the exposure of children to language that describes, in terms patently offensive as measured by contemporary community standards for the broadcast medium, sexual or excretory activities and organs, at times of the day when there is a reasonable risk that children may be in the audience." *Id.* at 732. *See*, note 62, *supra*.

18 *Id.* at 748-749.

19 *Id.* at 750.

Furthermore, the Commission "never intended to place an absolute prohibition on the broadcast of this type of language, but rather sought to channel it to times of day when children most likely would not be exposed to it."[20]

In 1988, Congress enacted P.L. 100-459, § 608, which required the FCC to promulgate regulations to ban indecent broadcasts 24 hours a day. The FCC did so, but the regulations never took effect because the court of appeals declared the ban unconstitutional because "the Commission may not ban such broadcasts entirely."[21] In 1992, Congress enacted P.L. 102-356, § 16 of which required the FCC to promulgate regulations that prohibit broadcasting of indecent programming on radio and television from 6 a.m. to midnight, except for *public* radio and television stations that go off the air at or before midnight, which may broadcast such material beginning at 10 p.m. 47 U.S.C. § 303 note. In 1993, a three-judge panel of the U.S. Court of Appeals for the District of Columbia held the law unconstitutional, but, on June 30, 1995, the full court of appeals, by a 7-4 vote, overturned the panel and upheld the statute, except for its 10 p.m.-to-midnight ban imposed on non-public stations.[22]

The court of appeals found "that the Government has a compelling interest in supporting parental supervision of what children see and hear on the public airwaves,"[23] and "that the Government has an independent and compelling interest in preventing minors from being exposed to indecent broadcasts."[24] The court found, in addition, that the statute used the least restrictive means to serve these interests.[25] However, the court found that "Congress has failed to explain what, if any, relationship the disparate treatment accorded certain public stations bears to the compelling Government interest — or to any other legislative value — that Congress

20 *Id.* at 733 (quoting the FCC).

21 Action for Children's Television v. Federal Communications Commission (ACT II), 932 F.2d 1504, 1509 (D.C. Cir. 1991), *cert. denied*, 503 U.S. 913 (1992).

22 Action for Children's Television v. Federal Communications Commission (ACT III), 58 F.3d 654 (D.C. Cir. 1995) (en banc), *cert. denied*, 516 U.S. 1043 (1996).

23 *Id.* at 661.

24 *Id.* at 663.

25 The court wrote: "While we apply strict scrutiny to regulations of this kind regardless of the medium affected by them, our assessment of whether section 16(a) survives that scrutiny must necessarily take into account the unique context of the broadcast media." *Id.* at 660. Chief Judge Edwards, in his dissent, wrote: "This is the heart of the case, plain and simple," as "[t]he majority appears to recognize that section 16(a) could not withstand constitutional scrutiny if applied against *cable* television operators." *Id.* at 671.

sought to advance when it enacted section 16(a)."[26] The court therefore held "that the section is unconstitutional insofar as it bars the broadcasting of indecent speech between the hours of 10:00 p.m. and midnight."[27]

Section 1465

This section makes it a crime knowingly to transport in interstate or foreign commerce for the purpose of sale or distribution, any "obscene, lewd, lascivious, or filthy" material, "or any other matter of indecent or immoral character." It also makes it a crime knowingly to travel in interstate commerce, or to use any facility or means of interstate commerce, for the purpose of transporting obscene material in interstate or foreign commerce. Section 1465 should be read as limited by the *Miller* standard.[28] The President's message that accompanied the original proposal that became P.L. 100-690 states:

> The term "facility of commerce" would include such things as the federal interstate highway system, federally numbered highways, and interstate railroads, even if such facility were used only intrastate. The term "means of interstate commerce" would include motor vehicles, boats, and airplanes capable of carrying goods in interstate commerce. The new offense would be committed, for example, by transporting obscene material by truck via Interstate 95 from Richmond to Alexandria, Virginia, with the intent that at least part of it would then be sold to customers outside of Virginia.[29]

In 1994, in Memphis, Tennessee, Robert and Carleen Thomas, a husband and wife from Milpitas, California, were convicted and sentenced to prison under 18 U.S.C. § 1465 for transmitting obscenity, from California, over interstate phone lines through their members-only computer bulletin board. The Sixth Circuit affirmed, holding that 18 U.S.C. § 1465 applies to computer transmissions.[30] The defendants had also raised a First Amendment

---

26 *Id.* at 668.

27 *Id.* at 669. Note that the court struck down the 10 p.m.-to-midnight ban not because it failed strict scrutiny under the First Amendment, but because it applied only to non-public stations. Chief Judge Edwards, in his dissent, commented that "the majority appears to invite Congress to extend the 6 a.m. to midnight ban to all broadcasters, without exception." *Id.* at 670 n.1.

28 United States v. Alexander, 498 F.2d 934, 935-936 (2d Cir. 1974).

29 H.R. Doc. No. 100-129, 100th Cong., 1st Sess. 78 (1987).

30 United States v. Thomas, 74 F.3d 701 (6th Cir. 1996), *cert. denied*, 519 U.S. 820 (1996). The court cited another conviction under 18 U.S.C. § 1465 for computer pornography — this one by an Air Force court. United States v. Maxwell, 42 M.J. 568 (A.F.Ct.Crim. App. 1995).

issue, arguing that they "cannot select who gets the materials they make available on their bulletin boards. Therefore, they contend, BBS [bulletin board service] operators like Defendants will be forced to censor their materials so as not to run afoul of the standards of the community with the most restrictive standards."[31] The court did not decide the issue because it found that, in this case, the defendants had transmitted only to members whose addresses they knew, so "[i]f Defendants did not wish to subject themselves to liability in jurisdictions with less tolerant standards for determining obscenity, they could have refused to give passwords to members in those districts, thus precluding the risk of liability."[32]

In 1996, P.L. 104-104, § 507(b), amended 18 U.S.C. § 1465 to apply to any "interactive computer service."

Section 1466

This section makes it a crime for any person "engaged in the business of selling or transferring obscene matter" knowingly to receive or possess with intent to distribute any obscene material that has been transported in interstate or foreign commerce. Offering to sell or transfer, at one time, two or more copies of any obscene publication, or a combined total of five, shall create a rebuttable presumption that the person so offering them is "engaged in the business." In other words, if the government proved that the defendant had offered to sell, at one time, two or more copies of any obscene publication, or a combined total of five, then the defendant would be deemed to be "engaged in the business" unless he could prove otherwise.

Section 1467

This section provides for criminal forfeiture in obscenity cases. Specifically, it provides that a person convicted under the federal obscenity statute (18 U.S.C. §§ 1460-1469) shall forfeit to the United States (1) the

[31] *Id.* at 711. In *Reno v. American Civil Liberties Union, supra* note 12, the Supreme Court noted that "the 'community standards' criterion as applied to the Internet means that any communication available to a nation-wide audience will be judged by the standards of the community most likely to be offended by the message." In *Ashcroft v. American Civil Liberties Union, infra* note 116, the Supreme Court held that the use of community standards to assess "harmful to minors" material on the Internet is not by itself unconstitutional.

[32] *Id.*

obscene material, (2) property traceable to gross profits or other proceeds obtained from the obscene material, (3) property used or intended to be used to commit the offense, "if the court in its discretion so determines, taking into consideration the nature, scope, and proportionality of the use of the property in the offense." Thus, the court must determine, for example, whether a vehicle used to transport obscene material was owned by the defendant and was frequently used for that purpose, or, on the other hand, whether it had been borrowed from someone who had no knowledge of the use to which the defendant intended to put it.

The right of the United States to the property vests upon violation of the obscenity statute, not upon conviction. Therefore, property that was transferred between the violation and the conviction belongs to the United States, and shall also be forfeited. However, the statute contains an exception precluding forfeiture if the person to whom the property was transferred establishes that at the time of purchase he "was reasonably without cause to believe that the property was subject to forfeiture." Thus, if a person is convicted and the money he paid his lawyer to defend him can be traced to gross profits from the sale of obscene material, the lawyer may be required to forfeit the money unless he can convince the court that he had no reasonable cause to believe that the money was subject to forfeiture.[33] The Supreme Court has held that forfeiture of lawyers' fees under the federal drug forfeiture statute does not violate the Due Process Clause of the Fifth Amendment or criminal defendants' Sixth Amendment right to counsel of choice.[34]

Section 1467(c) provides that, prior to conviction, upon application of the United States, a court may issue an *ex parte* restraining order or injunction "to preserve the availability of property ... for forfeiture." Section 1467(d) authorizes courts to issue warrants for the seizure of property solely upon a showing of "probable cause to believe that the property to be seized would, in the event of conviction, be subject to forfeiture and that an order under subsection (c) of this section may not be sufficient to assure the availability of the property for forfeiture." A federal district court declared these provisions unconstitutional insofar as they allow "seizure or restraint ...

[33] The lawyer could argue that the money came from a source independent of his client's alleged criminal activity; it seems less certain whether he could argue that, at the time his client paid him, he (the lawyer) was reasonably without cause to believe that the money was subject to forfeiture because he reasonably believed that his client would be found not guilty.

[34] Caplin & Drysdale v. United States, 491 U.S. 617 (1989).

without a prior adversarial hearing."[35] The court based this holding on the Supreme Court's decision in *Fort Wayne Books*, which is discussed in the section on RICO, below.

The court also declared two aspects of the post-conviction criminal forfeiture provisions unconstitutional. However, on appeal, the court of appeals, without addressing its merits, vacated the entire decision on the ground that, because the government had not threatened the plaintiffs with enforcement, the plaintiffs' claims were not ripe for judicial resolution.[36]

Section 1468

This section, enacted in 1988, makes it a crime "knowingly to utter[ ] obscene language or distribute[ ] any obscene matter by means of cable television or subscription services on television." Similarly, 47 U.S.C. § 559, enacted in 1984, makes it a crime to "transmit[ ] over any cable system any matter which is obscene or otherwise unprotected by the Constitution of the United States." The President's message that accompanied the original proposal that became section 1468 explained that the reason for its enactment was that ambiguities in Title 47 of the U.S. Code made it "unclear under what circumstances, if any, the federal government could enforce [47 U.S.C. § 559]."[37]

Section 1468 also provides that no provision of federal law is intended to preempt the power of the states, including their political subdivisions, "to regulate the uttering of language that is obscene or otherwise unprotected by the Constitution or the distribution of matter that is obscene or otherwise unprotected by the Constitution."

There are also other statutes codified in title 47 of the U.S. Code that regulate obscenity and indecency on cable television; see below.

Section 1469

This section creates a rebuttable presumption that an item produced in one state and subsequently located in another, or produced outside the United States and subsequently located in the United States, was transported

---

35 American Library Association v. Thornburgh, 713 F. Supp. 469, 485 (D.D.C. 1989), *vacated sub nom.* American Library Association v. Barr, 956 F.2d 1178 (D.C. Cir. 1992).

36 *Id.* at 1196.

37 H.R. Doc. No. 100-129, *supra* note 82, at 93.

in interstate or foreign commerce. This means that, if the government proves the change of location, then, unless the defendant shows that the allegedly obscene material had not been transported in interstate or foreign commerce, it would be deemed to have been so transported.

Section 1470

This section, added by P.L. 105-314, § 401 (1998), makes it a crime to use the mail or interstate or foreign commerce knowingly to transfer obscene matter to a person under 16, knowing that such person is under 16.

D. Cable Television

In addition to 18 U.S.C. § 1468 and 47 U.S.C. § 559 (discussed above under "Section 1468"), both of which prohibit obscenity on cable television, various provisions in the Communications Act of 1934, codified in title 47 of the U.S. Code, regulate obscenity and indecency on cable television.

In 1994, in *Turner Broadcasting System v. Federal Communications Commission*, which did not involve obscenity or indecency, the Supreme Court held that cable television is entitled to full First Amendment protection.[38] It wrote in *Turner*: "In light of these fundamental technological differences between broadcast and cable transmission, application of the more relaxed standard of scrutiny, adopted in *Red Lion* and other broadcast cases is inapt when determining the First Amendment validity of cable regulation."[39] In 1996, in *Denver Area Educational Telecommunications Consortium, Inc. v. Federal Communications Commission*, a plurality of the Justices retreated from the Court's position in *Turner*. They wrote: "The Court's distinction in *Turner*, ... between cable and broadcast television, relied on the inapplicability of the spectrum scarcity problem to cable... . While that distinction was relevant in *Turner* to the justification for structural regulations at issue there (the 'must carry' rules), it has little to do with a case that involves the effects of television viewing on children."[40]

In Part II of the *Denver Consortium* opinion, a plurality (four justices) upheld § 10(a) of the Cable Television Consumer Protection and

38 512 U.S. 622 (1994).

39 *Id.* at 639.

40 518 U.S. 727, 748 (1996).

Competition Act of 1992, 47 U.S.C. § 532(h), which permits cable operators to prohibit indecent material on leased access channels.[41] In upholding § 10(a), the Court, citing *Pacifica*, noted that cable television "is as 'accessible to children' as over-the-air broadcasting," has also "established a uniquely pervasive presence in the lives of all Americans," and can also "'confron[t] the citizen' in 'the privacy of the home,' ... with little or no prior warning."[42] Applying something less than strict scrutiny, the Court concluded "that § 10(a) is a sufficiently tailored response to an extraordinarily important problem."[43] It also found that "the statute is not impermissibly vague."[44]

In Part III of *Denver Consortium*, a majority (six justices) struck down § 10(b) of the 1992 Act, 47 U.S.C. § 532(j), which required cable operators, if they do not prohibit such programming on leased access channels, to segregate it on a single channel and block that channel unless the subscriber requests access to it in writing. In this part of the opinion, the Court appeared to apply strict scrutiny, finding "that protection of children is a 'compelling interest,'" but "that, not only is [§ 10(b)] not a 'least restrictive alternative,' and is not 'narrowly tailored' to meet its legitimate objective, it also seems considerably 'more extensive than necessary.'"[45]

In Part IV, which only three justices joined, the Court struck down § 10(c), 42 U.S.C. § 531 note, which permitted cable operators to prohibit indecent material on public access channels. Without specifying the level of scrutiny they were applying, the justices concluded "that the Government cannot sustain its burden of showing that §10(c) is necessary to protect children or that it is appropriately tailored to secure that end."[46]

Another relevant statute concerning cable television is 47 U.S.C. § 544(d)(1), which provides that a franchising authority and a cable operator may specify, in granting or renewing a franchise, "that certain cable services shall not be provided or shall be provided subject to conditions, if such cable services are obscene or are otherwise unprotected by the Constitution of the United States." In addition, 47 U.S.C. § 544(d)(2)(A) provides: "In order to

---

41 The Cable Communications Policy Act of 1984, P.L. 98-549, had required cable operators to provide leased access and public access channels free of operator editorial control. 47 U.S.C. §§ 531(e), 532(c)(2). These two provisions were amended in 1996 by § 506 of the Communications Decency Act to permit cable operators to refuse to transmit "obscenity, indecency, or nudity."

42 *Denver Consortium*, *supra* note 93, 518 U.S., at 744-745.

43 *Id.* at 743.

44 *Id.* at 753.

45 *Id.* at 755.

46 *Id.* at 766. Two other justices concurred in the judgment that § 10(c) is invalid, but for different reasons.

restrict the viewing of programming which is obscene or indecent, upon the request of a subscriber, a cable operator shall provide (by sale or lease) a device by which the subscriber can prohibit viewing of a particular cable service during a period selected by that subscriber."

The Communications Decency Act of 1996, P.L. 104-104, which is known primarily for its provisions regulating computer-transmitted indecency, also contained provisions concerning cable television. Section 504 added § 640 to the Communications Act of 1934, 47 U.S.C. § 560, which provides:

> Upon request by a cable service subscriber, a cable operator shall, without charge, fully scramble or otherwise fully block the audio and video programming of each channel carrying such programming so that one not a subscriber does not receive it.

This section includes no restriction on the type of material that a subscriber may request to have blocked.

Section 505 added § 641, 47 U.S.C. § 561, which provides:

> (a) In providing sexually explicit adult programming or other programming that is indecent on any channel of its service primarily dedicated to sexually-oriented programming, a multichannel video programming distributor shall fully scramble or otherwise fully block the video and audio portion of such channel so that one not a subscriber does not receive it.
>
> (b) Until a multichannel video programming distributor complies with the requirement set forth in subsection (a), the distributor shall limit the access of children to the programming referred to in that subsection by not providing such programming during the hours of the day (as determined by the [Federal Communications] Commission) when a significant number of children are likely to be viewing it.

On May 22, 2000, the Supreme Court declared § 505 unconstitutional, making clear, as it had not in *Denver Consortium*, that strict scrutiny applies to content-based speech restrictions on cable television.[47] The Court noted that "[t]he purpose of § 505 is to shield children from hearing or seeing images resulting from signal bleed," which refers to images or sounds that come through to non-subscribers, even though cable operators have "used scrambling in the regular course of business, so that only paying customers

---

[47] United States v. Playboy Entertainment Group, Inc., 529 U.S. 803, 813 (2000). The decision was 5-4, with Justices Breyer, Rehnquist, O'Connor, and Scalia dissenting.

had access to certain programs."[48] Section 505 requires cable operators to implement more effective scrambling – to *fully* scramble or otherwise *fully* block programming so that non-subscribers do not receive it – or to "time channel," which, under an F.C.C. regulation meant to transmit the programming only from 10 p.m. to 6 a.m.

"To comply with the statute," the Court noted, "the majority of cable operators adopted the second, or 'time channeling,' approach.[49] The effect ... was to eliminate altogether the transmission of the targeted programming outside the safe harbor period [6 a.m. to 10 p.m.] in affected cable service areas. In other words, for two-thirds of the day no household in those service areas could receive the programming, whether or not the household or the viewer wanted to do so."[50] The Court also noted that "[t]he speech in question was not thought by Congress to be so harmful that all channels were subject to restriction. Instead, the statutory disability applies only to channels 'primarily dedicated to sexually-oriented programming.'"[51]

As "a content-based speech restriction," the Court wrote, § 505 "can stand only if it satisfies strict scrutiny... . [I]t must ... promote a compelling Government interest... . If a less restrictive alternative would serve the Government's purpose, the legislature must use that alternative." The Court did not explicitly say in this case that protecting children from sexually oriented signal bleed is a compelling interest, but assumed it, and addressed the question of whether § 505 constituted the least restrictive means to advance that interest.[52]

The Court noted that there is "a key difference between cable television and the broadcasting media, which is the point on which this case turns: Cable systems have the capacity to block unwanted channels on a

---

48 *Id.* at 806.

49 *Id.* They may have done so because fully blocking or fully scrambling "appears not be economical" (*id.* at 808) or because the technology is imperfect and cable operators attempting to fully block or fully scramble might have still been "faced with the possibility of sanctions for intermittent bleeding" (*id.* at 821).

50 *Id.* at 806-807.

51 *Id.* at 812.

52 The Court wrote: "Even upon the assumption that the Government has an interest in substituting itself for informed and empowered parents, its interest is not sufficiently compelling to justify this widespread restriction on speech." *Id.* at 825. The Court, in other words, while assuming that the government has a compelling interest in aiding parents in protecting their children from sexually oriented signal bleed, did not find that the government has a compelling interest in protecting children from such material when their parents allow it into the home. The Court also noted "the possibility that a graphic image could have a negative impact on a young child." *Id.* at 826. This suggests the possibility that the Court might not find a compelling interest in shielding older children from sexually oriented material.

household-by-household basis ... [T]argeted blocking enables the Government to support parental authority without affecting the First Amendment interests of speakers and willing listeners ... ."[53] Furthermore, targeted blocking is already required – by § 504 of the CDA, which, as noted above, requires cable operators, upon request by a cable service subscriber, to, without charge, fully scramble or otherwise fully block audio and video programming that the subscriber does not wish to receive. "When a plausible, less restrictive alternative is offered to a content-based speech restriction, it is the Government's obligation to prove that the alternative will be ineffective to achieve its goal. The Government has not met that burden here."[54] The Court concluded, therefore, that § 504, with adequate publicity to parents of their rights under it, constituted a less restrictive alternative to § 505.

One additional provision of the CDA affected cable television: § 506 amended 47 U.S.C. §§ 531(e) and 532(c)(2) to permit cable operators to refuse to transmit "obscenity, indecency, or nudity" on public access and leased access channels.[55]

E. THE COMMUNICATIONS DECENCY ACT OF 1996

The Communications Decency Act of 1996 (CDA) is Title V of the Telecommunications Act of 1996, P.L. 104-104. This report has previously noted amendments the Act made to 18 U.S.C. §§ 1462 and 1465, and provisions relating to cable television that it added to Title 47 of the U.S. Code. This section of the report examines § 502 of the Act, which would have limited indecent material transmitted by telecommunications devices and interactive computer services, and *Reno v. American Civil Liberties Union*, 521 U.S. 844 (1997), the Supreme Court decision holding it unconstitutional.

Section 502 rewrote 47 U.S.C. § 223(a) and added subsections (d) through (h) to 47 U.S.C. § 223. It did not amend subsections (b) or (c), which restrict commercial dial-a-porn services (see page 10, above). In *Reno*, the Supreme Court struck down § 223(a) in part and § 223(d) in whole.

---

[53] *Id.* at 815.

[54] *Id.* at 816.

[55] Justice Kennedy, in the only footnote to his concurring and dissenting opinion in *Denver Consortium*, wrote that the constitutionality of the amendments made by § 506, "to the extent they differ from the provisions here [§§ 10(a) and 10(c) of the 1992 Act], is not before us." 518 U.S., at 782.

47 U.S.C. § 223(a)

Section 223(a)(1)(A) makes it a crime, by means of a telecommunications device, knowingly to transmit a communication that is "obscene, lewd, lascivious, filthy, indecent, with intent to annoy, abuse, threaten, or harass another person." Section 223(a)(1)(B) makes it a crime, by means of a telecommunications device, knowingly to transmit a communication that is "obscene or indecent, knowing that the recipient of the communication is under 18 years of age... ." Section 223(a)(2) makes it a crime knowingly to permit any telecommunications facility under one's control to be used for any activity prohibited by § 223(a)(1) with the intent that it be used for such activity.[56]

Although the CDA defines "telecommunications,"[57] it does not define "telecommunications device." However, it provides in § 223(h)(1)(B) that the term "does not include the use of an interactive computer service."[58] Thus, it appears that § 223(a)(1)(A) and (B) are intended to apply to communications, by telephone, fax machine, or computer, that are sent to particular individuals, not those that can be accessed by multiple users.

In *Reno v. American Civil Liberties Union*, the Supreme Court declared § 223(a)(1)(B) unconstitutional insofar as it applies to "indecent" communications.

---

56 In *ApolloMedia Corp. v. Reno*, 19 F. Supp.2d 1081, 1084 (N.D. Cal. 1998), *aff'd*, 526 U.S. 1061 (1999), the plaintiff sought to enjoin enforcement of § 223(a)(1)(A) and § 223(a)(2) "on the grounds that ... , to the extent that they prohibit 'indecent' communications made 'with an intent to annoy,' [they] are impermissibly overbroad and vague... ." The three-judge court denied the plaintiff's request because it found that "the provisions regulate only 'obscene' communications." The Supreme Court affirmed without a written opinion. The plaintiffs reportedly had appealed because they believed that the fact that the word "indecent" was in the statute could have a chilling effect on indecent nonobscene expression, even if the law was not enforceable against such expression.

57 Section 3 of P.L. 104-104 added to 47 U.S.C. § 153 the following definition of "telecommunications": "the transmission, between or among points specified by the user, of information of the user's choosing, without change in the format or content of the information as sent and received." The conference report adds that this information includes "voice, data, image, graphics, and video."

58 Section 230(f)(2) (added by § 509) defines "interactive computer service" as "any information service, system, or access software provider that provides or enables computer access by multiple users to a computer server, including specifically a service or system that provides access to the Internet and such systems operated or services offered by libraries or educational institutions."

47 U.S.C. § 223(d)

Section 223(d) makes it a crime knowingly to use "an interactive computer service to send to a specific person or persons under 18 years of age, or ... to display in a manner available to a person under 18 years of age, any ... communication that, in context, depicts or describes, in terms patently offensive as measured by contemporary community standards, sexual or excretory activities or organs ... ." This prohibition seems equivalent to a prohibition of "indecent" material, but § 223(d) does not use the word "indecent," a fact of which the Supreme Court took note in *Reno* when it held § 223(d) unconstitutional. *See*, 521 U.S., at 871.

Reno v. American Civil Liberties Union

The Supreme Court found in this case that "the CDA is a content-based blanket restriction on speech ... ." 521 U.S., at 868. As such, it may be found constitutional only if it serves "to promote a compelling interest" and is "the least restrictive means to further the articulated interest."[59] As for whether the CDA promotes a compelling interest, although the Court referred to "the legitimacy and importance of the congressional goal of protecting children from harmful materials" (521 U.S., at 849), it suggested that there may be less of a governmental interest in protecting older children from indecent material — at least such material as had artistic or educational value. *See*, 521 U.S., at 878.

As for whether the CDA is the least restrictive means to further the governmental interest, the Court found that "the Government [failed] to explain why a less restrictive provision would not be as effective as the CDA," 521 U.S., at 879. The CDA's "burden on adult speech," the Court held, "is unacceptable if less restrictive alternatives would be at least as effective in achieving the legitimate purpose that the statute was enacted to serve." *Id.* at 874. "[T]he Government may not 'reduc[e] the adult population ... to ... only what is fit for children.'" *Id.* at 875.

Could Congress reenact the CDA be reenacted in a narrower form that would be constitutional? The Supreme Court did not say, but it did not foreclose the possibility. It wrote:

---

59 *Sable*, *supra* note 4.

> The arguments in this Court have referred to possible alternatives such as requiring that indecent material be "tagged" in a way that facilitates parental control of material coming into their homes, making exceptions for messages with artistic or educational value, providing some tolerance for parental choice, and regulating some portions of the Internet — such as commercial web sites — differently from others, such as chat rooms.

521 U.S., at 879.

F. CHILD ONLINE PROTECTION ACT

On October 21, 1998, President Clinton signed into law the Omnibus Appropriations Act for fiscal year 1999 (P.L. 105-277), title XIV of which is the Child Online Protection Act (COPA). This law was an attempt to enact a constitutional version of the CDA. It differs from the CDA in two main respects: (1) it prohibits communication to minors only of material that is "harmful to minors," rather than material that is indecent, and (2) it applies only to communications for commercial purposes on publicly accessible Web sites. It defines "material that is harmful to minors" as pictures or words that —

> (A) the average person, applying contemporary community standards, would find, taking the material as a whole and with respect to minors, is designed to appeal to, or is designed to pander to, the prurient interest;
> (B) depicts, describes, or represents, in a manner patently offensive with respect to minors, an actual or simulated sexual act or sexual contact, an actual or simulated normal or perverted sexual act, or a lewd exhibition of the genitals or post-pubescent female breast; and
> (C) taken as a whole, lacks serious literary, artistic, political, or scientific value for minors.[60]

A communication is deemed to be for "commercial purposes" if it is made in the regular course of a trade or business with the objective of earning a profit; a communication need not propose a commercial transaction to be deemed to be for "commercial purposes." Requiring a viewer to use a credit card to gain access to material on the Internet would constitute a defense to prosecution.

---

[60] Despite the fact that only the first prong of this test refers to "community standards," community standards are apparently also intended to be used in applying the second prong. See footnote 7 of the Supreme Court's opinion, *infra* note 116.

In light of the Supreme Court's decision in *Reno*, is the Child Online Protection Act constitutional? The fact that COPA makes exceptions for messages with serious literary, artistic, political, or scientific value for minors, and that it applies only to commercial Web sites, makes it more likely than the CDA to be upheld. Nevertheless it may well, like the CDA, be found to "suppress[ ] a large amount of speech that adults have a constitutional right to receive and to address to one another."[61] This is because a Web site that is freely accessible, but is deemed "commercial" because it seeks to make a profit through advertisements, would apparently have to stop making its Web site freely accessible, or, in the alternative, would have to remove all words and pictures that might be deemed "harmful to minors" "by the standards of the community most likely to be offended by the message."[62]

COPA was scheduled to take effect on November 20, 1998, but a coalition of 17 civil liberties groups filed suit challenging it, and, on November 19, Judge Reed of the federal district court in Philadelphia, finding that there was a likelihood that the plaintiffs would prevail, issued a temporary restraining order against enforcement of the law. On February 1, 1999, he issued a preliminary injunction against enforcement pending a trial on the merits.[63] The preliminary injunction applies to all Internet users (not just the plaintiffs in this case) and provides that, even if the law is ultimately upheld, the Administration may not prosecute online speakers retroactively. On June 22, 2000, the U.S. Court of Appeals for the Third Circuit upheld the preliminary injunction, as it was "confident that the ACLU's attack on COPA's constitutionality is likely to succeed on the merits."[64] On May 13, 2002, the Supreme Court vacated the Third Circuit's opinion and remanded the case for further proceedings. It did not, however, remove the preliminary injunction against enforcement of the statute. Finally, on March 6, 2003, the Third Circuit again affirmed the district court's preliminary injunction. We now consider these four opinions in turn.

In issuing the preliminary injunction, the district court found that "[i]t is clear that Congress has a compelling interest in the protection of minors,

---

61 *Reno, supra* note 12, 521 U.S., at 874.

62 *Id.* at 877-878. In support of the law's constitutionality, one might analogize its restriction on speech to state law bans on "public display and unattended sale, in places where minors might be present, of 'obscene-as-to-minors' materials." *See*, Eugene Volokh, *Freedom of Speech, Shielding Children, and Transcending Balance*, 1997 SUP. CT. REV. 141, 186.

63 American Civil Liberties Union v. Reno, 31 F. Supp.2d 473 (E.D. Pa. 1999), *aff'd*, 217 F.3d 162 (3d Cir. 2000), *vacated and remanded sub nom.* Ashcroft v. American Civil Liberties Union, 122 S. Ct. 1700 (2002), *aff'd on remand*, 2033 WL 755083 (3d Cir., Mar. 6, 2003).

64 *Id.*, 217 F.3d, at 166.

including shielding them from materials that are not obscene by adult standards."[65] It also found, however, that "it is not apparent to this Court that the defendant can meet its burden to prove that COPA is the least restrictive means available to achieve the goal of restricting the access of minors to this material."[66] This is because "[t]he record before the Court reveals that blocking or filtering technology may be at least as successful as COPA would be in restricting minors' access to harmful material online without imposing the burden on constitutionally protected speech that COPA imposes on adult users or Web site operators."[67] In addition, "the sweeping category of forms of content that are prohibited — '*any communication*, picture, image, graphic image file, article, recording, *writing*, or *other matter of any kind*' (emphasis added [by the court]) — could have been less restrictive of speech on the Web and more narrowly tailored to Congress' goal of shielding minors from pornographic teasers if the prohibited forms of content had included, for instances, only pictures, images, or graphic image files, which are typically employed by adult entertainment Web sites as 'teasers.' In addition, perhaps the goals of Congress could be served without the imposition of possibly excessive and serious criminal penalties, including imprisonment and hefty fines, for communicating speech that is protected as to adults or without exposing speakers to prosecution and placing the burden of establishing an affirmative defense on them instead of incorporating the substance of the affirmative defenses in the elements of the crime."[68]

On appeal, the Third Circuit affirmed on a different ground: "because the standard by which COPA gauges whether material is 'harmful to minors' is based on identifying 'contemporary community standards' the inability of Web publishers to restrict access to their Web sites based on the geographic locale of the site visitor, in and of itself, imposes an impermissible burden on constitutionally protected First Amendment speech."[69] This is because it results in communications available to a nationwide audience being judged by the standards of the community most likely to be offended. Applying strict scrutiny, the Third Circuit concluded that, though "[i]t is undisputed that the government has a compelling interest in protecting children from material that is harmful to them, even if not obscene by adult standards,"[70] the government "may not regulate at all if it turns out that even the least

[65] *Id.*, 31 F. Supp.2d, at 495.
[66] *Id.* at 497.
[67] *Id.*
[68] *Id.*
[69] *Id.*, 217 F.3d, at 166.

restrictive means of regulation is still unreasonable when its limitations on freedom of speech are balanced against the benefits gained from those limitations."[71]

The Supreme Court held that COPA's "use of 'community standards' to identify 'material that is harmful to minors' ... does not render the statute facially unconstitutional" – it "does not *by itself* render the statute substantially overbroad for purposes of the First Amendment."[72] Although there were five separate opinions in the case, eight of the nine justices favored remanding the case to the Third Circuit to consider whether the Act was nevertheless unconstitutional. Only Justice Stevens dissented, as only he believed that the use of community standards was a sufficient problem to warrant an affirmance of the Third Circuit's opinion.

The Court's statement that COPA's use of community standards does not *by itself* render the statute unconstitutional implies that COPA's use of community standards may nevertheless prove a factor among others that renders the statute unconstitutional. Justice Thomas, however, despite writing the opinion for the Court, including the *by itself* language quoted above, wrote, in a section of the opinion joined only by Chief Justice Rehnquist and Justice Scalia, "that any variance caused by the statute's reliance on community standards is not substantial enough to violate the First Amendment."[73] Justice Thomas also commented: "If a publisher wishes for its material to be judged only by the standards of particular communities [and not by the most puritanical community], then it need only take the simple step of utilizing a medium [a medium other than the Internet] that enables it to target the release of its materials into those communities."[74] Justice Stevens responded that the Court should "place the burden on parents to 'take the simple step of utilizing a medium that enables' ... them to avoid this material before requiring the speaker to find another forum."[75]

Justice Kennedy, in a concurring opinion joined by Justices Souter and Ginsburg, found that "[w]e cannot know whether variation in community standards renders the Act substantially overbroad without first assessing the extent of speech covered and the variations in community standards with respect to that speech."[76] Justice Kennedy believed that, before an

---

70 *Id.* at 173.

71 *Id.* at 179.

72 122 S. Ct. 1700, 1713 (2002) (emphasis in original).

73 *Id.*

74 *Id.* at 1712.

75 Id. at 1724 n.2.

76 *Id.* at 1720.

assessment could be made, the Third Circuit should consider such questions as how much material COPA prohibits, how much the standard of the most puritanical community in the nation differ from standards of other communities, "what it means to evaluate Internet material 'as a whole,'" and the number of venues in which the government could prosecute violations of the Act.[77]

Justices O'Connor and Breyer wrote separate concurring opinions. Justice O'Connor agreed with Justice Kennedy that the plaintiffs had failed "to demonstrate substantial overbreadth due solely to the variation between local communities,"[78] and Justice Breyer, to avoid a First Amendment problem, would have construed the phrase "community standard" in the statute to mean a national standard.

On remand, the Third Circuit again affirmed the district court's preliminary injunction. It held "that the following provisions of COPA are not narrowly tailored to achieve the Government's compelling interest in protecting minors from harmful material and therefore fail the strict scrutiny test: (a) the definition of 'material that is harmful to minors,' ... (b) the definition of 'commercial purposes,' ... and (c) the '*affirmative defenses*' available to publishers, which require the technological screening of users for the purpose of age verification" (emphasis in original).

As for the definition of "material that is harmful to minors," the court found that the requirement that material be judged "as a whole" in determining whether it was designed to appeal to the prurient interests of minors and to lack serious value for minors meant "that each individual communication, picture, image, exhibit, etc. be deemed 'a whole' by itself ..., rather than in context." Yet "one sexual image, which COPA may proscribe as harmful material, might not be deemed to appeal to the prurient interest of minors if it were to be viewed in the context of an entire collection of Renaissance artwork." The court also found the word "minor" in the definition of "material that is harmful to minors" to be "not narrowly drawn to achieve the statute's purpose," because it precludes Web publishers from knowing whether "an infant, a five-year old, or a person just shy of age seventeen ... should be considered in determining whether the content of their Web site has 'serious ... value for [those] minors'" or "will trigger the prurient interest, or be patently offensive with respect to those minors ... ."

As for the definition of "commercial purposes," the court was "satisfied that COPA is not narrowly tailored to proscribe commercial pornographers

77 *Id.* at 1721.

78 *Id.* at 1715.

and their ilk, as the Government contends, but instead prohibits a wide range of protected expression." As for the affirmative defense available to publishers, the court found that it "will likely deter many adults from accessing restricted content, because many Web users are simply unwilling to provide identification information in order to gain access to content ... ."

The Third Circuit also found that voluntary "blocking and filtering techniques ... may be substantially less restrictive than COPA in achieving COPA's objective of preventing a minor's access to harmful material." Finally, if held "that the plaintiffs will more probably prove at trial that COPA is substantially overbroad, and therefore, we will affirm the District Court on this independent ground as well."

G. Children's Internet Protection Act

The Children's Internet Protection Act (CIPA), P.L. 106-554 (2000), amended three federal statutes to provide that a school or library may not use funds it receives under these statutes to purchase computers used to access the Internet, or to pay the direct costs of accessing the Internet, and may not receive universal service discounts (other than for telecommunications services), unless the school or library enforces a policy "that includes the operation of a technology protection measure" that blocks or filters minors' Internet access to visual depictions that are obscene, child pornography, or harmful to minors; and that blocks or filters adults' Internet access to visual depictions that are obscene or child pornography.[79] CIPA's effective date was April 20, 2001 (120 days after the date of enactment), but its enforcement against libraries was enjoined by a three-judge federal district court in a decision we discuss below.

The sections of CIPA (1711 and 1712) that require schools and libraries to block or filter if they use federal funds for computers or for Internet access, provide that the blocking or filtering technology may be disabled "to enable access for bona fide research or other lawful purpose." But, as obscenity, child pornography, and material that is "harmful to minors"

[79] Section 1711 amends Title III of the Elementary and Secondary Education Act of 1965, 20 U.S.C. §§ 6801 *et seq*. Section 1712 amends section 224 of the Museum and Library Services Act, 20 U.S.C. § 9134, which is part of the Library Services and Technology Act (LSTA), which is Title II of the Museum and Library Services Act. Section 1721 amends section 254(h) of the Communications Act of 1934, 47 U.S.C. § 254(h), which establishes the "universal service discount," or "E-rate," for schools and libraries. Only sections 1712 and 1721 (insofar as it applies to libraries) were at issue in the case before the three-judge district court.

(insofar as it is distributed to minors), are all generally unlawful, it is unclear what effect this provision will have.

The section of CIPA (1721) that requires schools and libraries to block or filter if they receive universal service discounts, provides that the blocking or filtering technology may be disabled "during use by an adult, to enable access for bona fide research or other lawful purpose." As obscenity and child pornography are generally unlawful, this provision apparently authorizes the disabling, during use by an adult, only of technology that blocks or filters material that is "harmful to minors." Yet the statute does not require, as to adults, blocking or filtering of material that is "harmful to minors," so it is not clear why a provision authorizing disabling was included – perhaps it covers situations where a school or library has only one computer and therefore must block material that is "harmful to minors" as to both minors and adults.

Sections 1711, 1712, and 1721 all contain identical definitions of "minor," "obscene," "child pornography," and "harmful to minors." They define a "minor" as a person under 17. They define "obscene" to have the meaning given such term in18 U.S.C. § 1460, but that section does not define "obscene."[80] In the absence of a statutory definition, the courts will no doubt apply the *Miller* test to define the word.

Sections 1711, 1712, and 1721 all define "child pornography" to have the meaning given such term in 18 U.S.C. § 2256. That section defines "child pornography" as any "visual depiction" of "sexually explicit conduct" that is or appears to be of a minor, and defines "sexually explicit conduct" as various "actual or simulated" sexual acts or the "lascivious exhibition of the genitals or pubic area of any person." Child pornography need not be obscene under the *Miller* test; it is unprotected by the First Amendment even if it does not appeal to the prurient interest, is not patently offensive, and does not lack serious literary, artistic, scientific, or political value.

Sections 1711, 1712, and 1721 define "material that is harmful to minors" as any communication that –

> (i) taken as a whole and with respect to minors, appeals to a prurient interest in nudity, sex, or excretion;
> (ii) depicts, describes, or represents, in a patently offensive way with respect to what is suitable for minors, an actual or simulated sexual act

[80] Nor does any other section of the U.S. Code, except 20 U.S.C. § 952(*l*), which defines it for purposes of grants by the National Endowment for the Arts, and does so in a manner that parallels the *Miller* test, except that it does not apply community standards to the determination of whether material is patently offensive.

or sexual contact, actual or simulated normal or perverted sexual acts, or a lewd exhibition of the genitals; and

(iii) taken as a whole, lacks serious literary, artistic, political, or scientific value as to minors.[81]

On May 31, 2002, in *American Library Association v. United States*, a three judge federal district court in Philadelphia unanimously declared CIPA unconstitutional and enjoined its enforcement insofar as it applies to libraries.[82] The government has a right to appeal directly to the U.S. Supreme Court, as CIPA, like the CDA but unlike COPA, prescribes this procedure. On November 12, 2002, the Court agreed to hear the case, and, on March 5, 2003, it heard arguments in the case.

The plaintiffs in this case alleged that CIPA was unconstitutional on its face and not merely as applied in particular circumstances. The court, therefore, "assume[d] without deciding, for purposes of this case, that ... plaintiffs [must] show that any public library that complies with CIPA will necessarily violate the First Amendment ... ."[83] It concluded that, "[b]ecause of the inherent limitations in filtering technology, public libraries can never comply with CIPA without blocking access to a substantial amount of speech that is ... constitutionally protected."[84] The court also found that "less restrictive alternatives exist that further the government's legitimate interest in preventing the dissemination of obscenity, child pornography, and material harmful to minors, and in preventing patrons from being unwillingly exposed to patently offensive, sexually explicit content."[85]

The court noted that "the plaintiffs demonstrated that thousands of Web pages containing protected speech are wrongly blocked by the four leading filtering programs, and these pages represent only a fraction of Web pages wrongly blocked by the programs... .[86] One failure of critical importance is

---

[81] This three-part test is similar to that of the Child Online Protection Act, 47 U.S.C. § 231(e), but three differences are that CIPA applies only to images, whereas COPA applies to images and words; CIPA does not, like COPA, provide that the prurience determination be made in accordance with the views of "the average person applying contemporary community standards"; and CIPA does not, like COPA, allow an image or description of the "post-pubescent female breast" to be found harmful to minors.

[82] 201 F. Supp.2d 401 (E.D. Pa. 2002), *prob. juris. noted*, 123 S. Ct. 551 (2002). The court struck down § 1712(a)(2), which concerns LSTA funds, and § 1721(b) which concerns Erate discounts for libraries. The provisions affecting schools were not challenged.

[83] *Id.* at 453.

[84] *Id.*

[85] *Id.* at 410.

[86] *Id.* at 408. At another point in its opinion, the court wrote: "At least tens of thousands of pages of the indexable Web are overblocked by each of the filtering programs evaluated by the experts in this case, even when considered against the filtering companies' own category

that the automated systems that filtering companies use to collect Web pages for classification are able to search only text, not images... . [W]e find that it is currently impossible, given the Internet's size, rate of growth, rate of change, and architecture, and given the state of the art of automated classification systems, to develop a filter that neither underblocks nor overblocks a substantial amount of speech."[87]

Does it make a difference that libraries can avoid CIPA's requirements by declining to accept LSTA funds or E-rate discounts? In *South Dakota v. Dole*, the Supreme Court held that Congress, incident to its power to provide for the general welfare (Art. I, § 8, cl. 1),

> may attach conditions on the receipt of federal funds, and has repeatedly employed the power "to further broad policy objectives by conditioning receipt of federal moneys upon compliance with federal statutory and administrative directives." ... The breadth of this power was made clear in *United States v. Butler*, 297 U.S. 1, 66 (1936), where the Court ... determined that "the power of Congress to authorize expenditure of public moneys for public purposes is not limited by the direct grants of legislative power found in the Constitution." Thus, objectives not thought to be within Article I's "enumerated legislative fields," *id.*, at 65, may nevertheless be attained through the use of the spending power and the conditional grant of federal funds.[88]

This means that Congress may regulate matters by attaching conditions to the receipt of federal funds that it might lack the power to regulate directly. The Court added, however, that "other constitutional provisions may provide an independent bar to the conditional grant of federal funds."[89] One of these other constitutional provisions is the First Amendment. The

definitions. Many erroneously blocked pages contain content that is completely innocuous for both adults and minors, and that no rational person could conclude matches the filtering companies' category definitions, such as 'pornography' or 'sex.'" *Id.* at 449.

87 At another point in its opinion, the court wrote: "No presently conceivable technology can make the judgments necessary to determine whether a visual depiction fits the legal definitions of obscenity, child pornography, or harmful to minors. Given the state of the art in filtering and image recognition technology, and the rapidly changing and expanding nature of the Web, we find that filtering products' shortcomings will not be solved through a technical solution in the foreseeable future." *Id.* at 449. The court might have added that it appears conceptually impossible for a computer program to determine whether, according to contemporary community standards, material appeals to the prurient interest or is patently offensive; whether it lacks serious literary, artistic, political, or scientific value; or whether a person who is pictured is over 18 or is real or "virtual." (The Supreme Court has held that non-obscene "virtual" child pornography is constitutionally protected speech. Ashcroft v. Free Speech Coalition, 122 S. Ct. 1389 (2002). See CRS Report 95-406 A.)

88 483 U.S. 203, 206-207 (1987).

89 *Id.* at 208.

Court has held, in fact, that the government "may not deny a benefit to a person on a basis that infringes his constitutionally protected interests – especially, his interest in freedom of speech."[90]

The CIPA court saw the question before it as "whether CIPA requires libraries that receive LSTA funds or E-rate discounts to violate the constitutional rights of their patrons."[91] To answer this question, the court first found that "[i]n providing even filtered Internet access, public libraries create a public forum open to any speaker around the world to communicate with library patrons via the Internet on a virtually unlimited number of topics."[92] The fact that CIPA would require public libraries that accept federal funds to impose content-based restrictions in public forums means that CIPA is subject to strict scrutiny. "Under strict scrutiny, a public library's use of filtering software is permissible only if it is narrowly tailored to further a compelling governmental interest and no less restrictive alternative would serve that interest."

The court suggested various less restrictive alternatives that could further the government's legitimate interests:

> To prevent patrons from accessing visual depictions that are obscene and child pornography, public libraries may enforce Internet use policies that make clear to patrons that the library's Internet terminals may not be used to access illegal speech. Libraries may then impose penalties on patrons who violate these policies, ranging from a warning to notification of law enforcement, in the appropriate case. Less restrictive alternatives to

---

90 Perry v. Sindermann, 408 U.S. 593, 597 (1972) (striking down state university's refusal to renew teacher's contract because of his public criticism of the college administration).

91 Because the court answered this question in the affirmative, it found that it "need not reach the plaintiffs' alternative theories that CIPA is invalid as a prior restraint on speech and is unconstitutionally vague. Nor need we decide whether CIPA is invalid because it requires public libraries, as a condition on the receipt of federal funds, to relinquish their own First Amendment rights to provide the public with unfiltered Internet access... ." 201 F. Supp.2d, at 490.

92 The court found that "the relevant forum for analysis is not the library's entire collection, which includes both print and electronic media, such as the Internet, but rather the specific forum created when the library provides its patrons with Internet access." *Id.* at 456. This is significant because a public library's print materials are not "a public forum open to any speaker around the world ... ." *Id.* at 409. "Thus, a public library's decision to use the last $100 of its budget to purchase the complete works of Shakespeare even though more of its patrons would prefer the library to use the same amount to purchase the complete works of John Grisham, is not, in our view, subject to strict scrutiny." *Id.* at 462. Public libraries' use of Internet filters is different because, "by providing patrons with even filtered Internet access, the library permits patrons to receive speech on a virtually unlimited number of topics, from a virtually unlimited number of speakers, without attempting to restrict patrons' access to speech that the library, in the exercise of its professional judgment, determines to be particularly valuable." *Id.*

filtering that further libraries' interests in preventing minors from exposure to visual depictions that are harmful to minors include requiring parental consent to or presence during unfiltered access, or restricting minors unfiltered access to terminals within view of library staff. Finally, optional filtering, privacy screens, recessed monitors, and placement of unfiltered Internet terminals outside of sight-lines provide less restrictive alternatives for libraries to prevent patrons from being unwillingly exposed to sexually explicit content on the Internet.

The court then considered whether CIPA's disabling provisions would cure its constitutional defect. It noted the provisions' lack of clarity, but "assume[d] without deciding that the disabling provisions permit libraries to allow a patron to access any speech that is constitutionally protected with respect to that patron [adult or minor]." Even under this broad interpretation, the court found, the disabling provisions do not save the statute. "By requiring library patrons affirmatively to request permission to access certain speech singled out on the basis of its content, CIPA will deter patrons from requesting that a library disable filters to allow the patron to access speech that is constitutionally protected, yet sensitive in nature... . [E]ven allowing anonymous requests for unblocking burdens patrons' access to speech, since such requests cannot immediately be acted on... . [R]equests sometimes are not reviewed for several days," and this "will, as a practical matter, impose a significant burden on library patrons' use of the Internet." As noted above, the court enjoined the enforcement of CIPA, as *American Library Association v. United States* awaits a decision by the Supreme Court.

H. RICO

The Federal Racketeer Influenced and Corrupt Organizations Act (RICO), was amended in 1984 to add the obscenity crimes specified in 18 U.S.C. §§ 1461-1465 to the definition of "racketeering activity" in 18 U.S.C. § 1961(1)(B). RICO makes it a crime for any person employed by or associated with any "enterprise" engaged in or affecting interstate or foreign commerce to participate in the affairs of the enterprise "through a pattern of racketeering activity." 18 U.S.C. § 1962(c). A "pattern of racketeering activity" means at least two acts of racketeering activity within ten years (excluding any period of imprisonment). 18 U.S.C. § 1961(5). Thus, if a person engages in two such activities, including the obscenity offenses specified, he is subject to prosecution under RICO in addition to, or instead of, prosecution for the particular activities.

RICO also provides for criminal forfeiture (18 U.S.C. § 1963), and its criminal forfeiture provision has been used in obscenity prosecutions; see *Alexander v. United States*, *infra*. In *Fort Wayne Books, Inc. v. Indiana*, 489 U.S. 46 (1989), the Supreme Court held that *pretrial* seizure, under the Indiana RICO statute, of books or other expressive materials, was unconstitutional. Although probable cause to believe that a person has committed a crime is sufficient to arrest him, "probable cause to believe that there are valid grounds for seizure is insufficient to interrupt the sale of presumptively protected books and films." *Id.* at 66. This presumption of First Amendment protection "is not rebutted until the claimed justification for seizing books or other publications is properly established in an adversary proceeding." *Id.* at 67. The Federal RICO statute, in any event, does not provide for pretrial seizure.[93]

In *Fort Wayne Books*, the Court did, however, uphold the constitutionality of including obscenity violations among the predicate offenses under a RICO statute. The Court rejected the argument "that the potential punishments available under the RICO law are so severe that the statute lacks a 'necessary sensitivity to first amendment rights.'" *Id.* at 57. Further, the Court held that such obscenity violations need not be "affirmed convictions on successive dates ... in the same jurisdiction as that where the RICO charge is brought." *Id.* at 61.

The fact that the violations need not be affirmed convictions means that the obscenity violations may be proved as part of the RICO prosecution; no "warning shot" in the form of a prior conviction for obscenity is required. "As long as the standard of proof is the proper one with respect to all the elements of the RICO allegation — including proof, beyond a reasonable doubt, of the requisite number of constitutionally-proscribable predicate acts — all of the relevant constitutional requirements have been met." *Id.*

The fact that the predicate offenses need not be convictions in the same jurisdiction as that where the RICO charge is brought means that the predicate offenses can be violations which were based on community standards different from those of the jurisdiction where the RICO charge is brought.[94] "But, as long as, for example, each previous obscenity conviction was measured by the appropriate community's standard, we see no reason why the RICO prosecution — alleging a pattern of such violations — may

[93] *See*, Fort Wayne Books, Inc. v. Indiana, 489 U.S., at 67 n.13.

[94] This could be the case even in a RICO prosecution based on predicate offenses in a different part of the same state, as the relevant community may be an area less than the entire state. *See*, Hamling v. United States, 418 U.S. 87, 105 (1974).

take place only in a jurisdiction where two or more such offenses have occurred." *Id.* at 62.[95]

In *Alexander v. United States*, the Supreme Court addressed a question it had left open in *Fort Wayne Books*: whether there are First Amendment limitations to RICO forfeitures of assets that consist of expressive materials that are otherwise protected by the First Amendment.[96] The defendant in the case had been found guilty of selling four magazines and three videotapes that were obscene, and, on that basis, had been convicted under RICO. He was sentenced to six years in prison, fined $100,000, and ordered to pay the cost of prosecution, incarceration, and supervised release. He was also ordered to forfeit all his wholesale and retail businesses, including more than a dozen stores and theaters dealing in sexually explicit material, all the assets of these businesses (*i.e.*, expressive materials, whether or not obscene), and almost $9 million. The government chose to destroy, rather than sell, the expressive material.

The Supreme Court rejected the argument that the forfeiture of expressive materials constitutes prior restraint, as the forfeiture order "does not *forbid* petitioner from engaging in any expressive activities in the future, nor does it require him to obtain prior approval for any expressive activities."[97] Consequently, the Court analyzed the forfeiture "under normal First Amendment standards," and could see no reason why, "if incarceration for six years and a fine of $100,000 are permissible forms of punishment under the RICO statute, the challenged forfeiture of certain assets directly related to petitioner's racketeering activity is not... . [T]he First Amendment does not prohibit either stringent criminal sanctions for obscenity offenses or forfeiture of expressive materials as punishment for criminal conduct."[98]

The Court did, however, remand the case to the court of appeals to decide whether the forfeiture constituted an "excessive fine" under the Eighth Amendment. The same day, in another case, the Court held that the Excessive Fines Clause of the Eighth Amendment applies to forfeitures of property imposed by criminal statutes.[99]

---

95 Although the Court uses the word "conviction" in this sentence, there appears to be no reason why a RICO prosecution could not be based on a violation in another jurisdiction that had not previously been prosecuted in that jurisdiction. In such a case, the prosecution would have to prove beyond a reasonable doubt that the laws (including, in an obscenity case, the community standards) of the state where the predicate offense occurred had been violated.

96 509 U.S. 544 (1993).

97 *Id.* at 550-551.

98 *Id.* at 554-555.

99 Austin v. United States, 509 U.S. 602 (1993).

I. WIRETAPS

P.L. 100-690, § 7525, amended 18 U.S.C. § 2516 to authorize federal judges to approve "the interception of wire or oral communications" to collect evidence of violations of the federal obscenity statute (18 U.S.C. §§ 1460-1469).

J. THE CUSTOMS SERVICE PROVISION

This statute, which is codified at 19 U.S.C. § 1305, prohibits importation of, among other things, obscene material, and provides, upon the appearance of any such material at a customs office, for its civil forfeiture. P.L. 100-690, § 7522(e),[100] amended 19 U.S.C. § 1305 to coordinate seizure by customs officers with criminal prosecutions under 18 U.S.C. § 1462. As the message of the President that accompanied the original proposal that became P.L. 100-690 explained, "While most obscene material seized by the Customs Service is forfeited under section 1305, some is of such a nature that it is referred for criminal prosecution as a violation of 18 U.S.C. 1462, importation of obscene material ... ."[101] The amendment to section 1305 provides:

> [W]henever the Customs Service is of the opinion that criminal prosecution is appropriate or that further criminal investigation is warranted in connection with allegedly obscene material seized at the time of entry, the appropriate customs officer shall immediately transmit information concerning such seizure to the United States Attorney of the district of the *addressee's* residence... .

The amendment then sets forth the subsequent procedures to be followed by the U.S. Attorney.

---

100 Subsection (e) apparently should have been "(d)," as there is no "(d)" following "(c)."

101 H.R. Doc. 100-129, *supra* note 76, at 82.

INDEX

A

B

C

D

E

S

T

U

Y